Cooking
with
Mum

igloobooks

Published in 2014
by Igloo Books Ltd
Cottage Farm
Sywell
NN6 0BJ
www.igloobooks.com

HUN001 0814
2 4 6 8 10 9 7 5 3 1
ISBN 978-1-78343-358-2

Food photography and recipe development:
PhotoCuisine UK

Front and back cover images:
PhotoCuisine UK

Printed and manufactured in China

Contents

Stuffed peppers

Pasta and meatballs in tomato sauce

Blueberry pancakes

Introduction

Enter the world of delicious and yummy cooking with this clear and simple recipe book. Cooking with Mum has never been so much fun!

Whether you are a beginner or you've been cooking for a while, there's lots of fun to be had in the kitchen. From tasty snacks to gourmet meals, finished off with mouth-watering desserts, you'll find recipes to suit everyone and every occasion, including tea parties, birthday treats, afternoon snacks and evening mealtimes.

Each recipe comes with simple, easy-to-follow steps and a stunning photograph, so you can see exactly what your dish will look like. With tasty recipes including homemade chips, mini pizzas, lasagne, soup, apple pie and muffins, you are spoilt for choice.

Don't forget to read the top tips that go with each recipe; these will help you on your way. Start off by reading the Golden Rules carefully on the next page.

Fresh tomato soup

Apple pie

Hazelnut and cinnamon muffins

Vegetable lasagne

Golden Rules

Before

1. Always ask an adult's permission before you start cooking, or ask them to help you.
2. Wash your hands before you start cooking and always after handling raw meat.
3. To keep your clothes clean, wear an apron.
4. Read through the recipe and check you have all of the ingredients and equipment required.
5. Measure your ingredients carefully.

During

1. Follow the step-by-step instructions, making sure you ask an adult for help if you don't understand something.
2. Wash fruit and vegetables to remove any dirt and chemicals.
3. Use a separate chopping board if you're cutting meat.
4. Take extra care with scissors or knives; ask an adult to teach you or to help.
5. Always make sure you remain in the kitchen during the cooking process and keep an eye on your dish.
6. Always use oven gloves and be careful when using the oven.

After

1. If you're baking, then remember to turn the oven off when you have finished.
2. Help clean the kitchen, tidy away the equipment and wash the dishes.
3. Enjoy eating your delicious creations.

Caesar Salad

Deep-fried Mozzarella

Light bites and snacks

Garlic bread with cheese

Coleslaw

Coleslaw

Serves: 8 Preparation time: 15 minutes

Ingredients

- 3 large carrots, peeled
- 1 small white cabbage
- 1 onion, peeled
- ½ lemon, juiced
- 350 ml / 12 fl. oz/ 1 ½ cups mayonnaise

- Coarsely grate the carrots and transfer them to a large mixing bowl.
- Cut the cabbage and onion into quarters then cut each quarter across into very thin slices.
- Mix the cabbage and onion with the grated carrot, breaking it up into individual strands with your fingers.
- Stir the lemon juice into the mayonnaise and use it to dress the shredded vegetables.
- Taste the coleslaw for seasoning, adding salt and pepper as necessary.

Top Tip

Add a few diced segments of citrus fruit such as grapefruit or tangerine for a more zesty taste.

Serve with burgers.

Top Tip

Add some finely chopped sun-dried tomatoes before the cheese for a more tangy taste.

Goes well with pasta.

Garlic Bread with Cheese

Serves: 6   Preparation time: 3 minutes   Cooking time: 5 minutes

Ingredients

- 75 g / 2 ½ oz / ⅓ cup butter, softened
- 1 clove of garlic, crushed
- ½ tsp dried herbs
- 1 large baguette, sliced
- 150 g / 5 ½ oz / ⅘ cup Gruyere cheese, grated

- Preheat the grill to its highest setting.

- Mix the butter with the garlic and herbs in a small bowl.

- Spread the baguette slices out on a large baking tray and toast them on one side under the grill.

- Turn the slices over and spread them with garlic butter then sprinkle over the grated cheese.

- Cook under the grill for 2 minutes or until the cheese is melted and the edges are starting to brown.

Mini Cheese Flatbreads

Makes: 32–36   Preparation time: 2 hours 30 minutes

Cooking time: 8–12 minutes

Ingredients

- 400 g / 14 oz / 3 ⅕ cups bread flour, plus extra for dusting
- ½ tsp easy blend dried yeast
- 1 tbsp caster sugar
- 1 tsp fine sea salt
- 2 tbsp olive oil

- 125 g / 4 ½ oz / ⅚ cup mozzarella, finely chopped
- 125 g / 4 ½ oz / ⅚ cup Cheddar, finely grated
- 2 tbsp flat leaf parsley, chopped

- In a large bowl, mix together the flour, yeast, sugar and salt. Stir the oil into 280 ml of warm water.

- Stir the liquid into the dry ingredients then knead the mixture on a lightly oiled surface with your hands for 10 minutes or until the dough is smooth and elastic.

- Leave the dough to rest in a lightly oiled bowl, covered with oiled clingfilm, for 1–2 hours or until doubled in size.

- Preheat the oven to 220°C (200°C fan) / gas 7 and grease 3 non-stick baking trays.

- Punch the dough with your fist to knock out the air then knead it for 2 minutes.

- Rub your fingers with a little olive oil then pull off a golf ball sized piece of dough and flatten it onto one of the baking trays with your hands.

- Repeat with the rest of the dough to make 32–36 flatbreads, each around 8 cm in diameter.

- Mix the mozzarella and Cheddar together and sprinkle it over the flatbreads.

- Bake for 8–12 minutes or until each bread is cooked through underneath and the cheese is bubbling.

- Sprinkle with parsley and serve warm.

Top Tip

Replace the parsley with 2 tbsp of chopped fresh basil for a more herby taste.

Perfect afternoon snack.

Delicious as a starter.

Deep-fried Mozzarella

Serves: 6   Preparation time: 30 minutes   Cooking time: 50 minutes

Ingredients

- 4 tbsp plain flour
- 1 egg, beaten
- 75 g / 2 ½ oz / 1 cup of breadcrumbs
- 4 mozzarella balls
- 2 litres / 3 ½ pints / 8 ½ cups sunflower oil

- Put the flour, egg and breadcrumbs in 3 separate bowls.
- Cut each mozzarella ball in half and dry well with kitchen paper.
- Dip each piece in the flour with one hand and pat off any excess, then drop them into the beaten egg.
- Take them out of the egg with your other hand and drop them into the breadcrumbs.

- Use your floury hand to move them around in the crumbs so that they are completely coated. If you stick to using one hand for wet and one hand for dry, you shouldn't get too messy.
- Heat the oil in a deep fat fryer, according to the manufacturer's instructions, to a temperature of 180°C.
- Lower the mozzarella halves in the fryer basket and cook for 4–5 minutes or until crisp and golden brown.
- Line a large bowl with a thick layer of kitchen paper and when they are ready, tip them into the bowl to remove any excess oil.
- Sprinkle with a little sea salt to taste and serve immediately.

Parmesan and Sesame Straws

Makes: 30–40   **Preparation time:** 10 minutes   **Cooking time:** 15–20 minutes

Ingredients

- 250 g / 9 oz all-butter puff pastry
- 1 egg, beaten
- 100 g / 3 ½ oz / 1 cup Parmesan, finely grated
- 1 tbsp sesame seeds
- 1 tbsp black sesame seeds

- Preheat the oven to 220°C (200°C fan) / 425F / gas 7 and line a baking tray with non-stick baking paper.
- Roll out the pastry on a floured surface into a large rectangle, checking regularly underneath to make sure it's not sticking.
- Brush the surface with egg and scatter over half of the Parmesan, then fold the pastry in half to enclose the cheese.

- Roll out the pastry again so that it is 5 mm thick then brush the top with more beaten egg and scatter over the rest of the Parmesan and the sesame seeds.
- Use a sharp knife to cut the sheet into short fingers and spread them out on the baking tray.
- Bake in the oven for 15–20 minutes or until they are golden brown and cooked through.
- Transfer the pastries to a wire rack to cool a little before serving warm.

Top Tip

Sprinkle a generous pinch of cayenne pepper when you roll in the cheese for a bit of extra kick.

Perfect treat for parties.

Top Tip

Sprinkle 3 tbsp of grated fresh Parmesan cheese into the mixture when cooking for a cheesy taste.

Delicious, hearty breakfast.

Scrambled Eggs with Mushrooms

Serves: 4   Preparation time: 10 minutes   Cooking time: 12 minutes

Ingredients

- 8 large eggs
- 2 tbsp tarragon leaves, chopped
- 2 tbsp butter
- 4 slices wholemeal toast

For the mushrooms:
- 10 g butter
- 150 g / 5 ¼ oz / 1 ¼ cups baby button mushrooms
- 1 tbsp tarragon leaves, chopped

- First prepare the mushrooms. Heat the butter in a large frying pan until it starts to sizzle then add the mushrooms.
- Fry for 10 minutes, stirring occasionally, until any liquid that comes out has evaporated and the mushrooms are golden brown. Sprinkle over the tarragon.

- Meanwhile, break the eggs into a jug with a pinch of salt and pepper and the chopped tarragon, then beat gently to break up the yolks.
- Heat the butter in a non-stick frying pan until sizzling then pour in the eggs.
- Cook over a low heat, stirring constantly until the eggs have scrambled.
- Divide the scrambled eggs between 4 slices of toast and top with the mushrooms.

Stuffed Peppers

Serves: 4   Preparation time: 10 minutes   Cooking time: 1 hour

Ingredients

- 4 red peppers
- 4 pork sausages
- 200 g / 7 oz / ⁴/₅ cup cooked rice, cooled
- 3 tbsp pitted black olives, chopped
- 250 g / 9 oz / cups mozzarella, cubed

- Preheat the oven to 180°C (160°C fan) / 350F / gas 4.

- Cut the tops off the peppers then pull out and discard the seeds and membrane inside.

- Squeeze the sausages out of their skins into a bowl and break up with a fork, then stir in the rice, olives and mozzarella cubes. Season with plenty of black pepper.

- Stuff the peppers with the rice mixture and put the lids back on, then arrange them in a roasting tin.

- Bake the peppers for 1 hour or until they are piping hot all the way through.

Top Tip

Mix 3 tbsp tomato puree into the sausage mixture for a more tangy flavour.

Tasty side dish.

Great for picnics.

Tomato Rarebit Tartlets

Makes: 6   *Preparation time:* 45 minutes   *Cooking time:* 35 minutes

Ingredients

- 25 g / 1 oz / ¹/₁₀ cup butter
- 25 g / 1 oz / ¹/₄ cup plain flour
- 125 ml / 4 ½ fl. oz ½ alcohol-free pale ale
- 2 tsp Worcestershire sauce
- 1 tsp Dijon mustard
- 125 g / 4 ½ oz / 1 ¹/₄ cup Cheddar

- 2 large tomatoes, sliced
- 2 tbsp pine nuts, chopped

For the pastry:
- 150 g / 5 ½ oz / ²/₃ cup butter, cubed
- 300 g / 10 ½ / 2 cups oz stoneground wholemeal flour

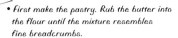

- First make the pastry. Rub the butter into the flour until the mixture resembles fine breadcrumbs.
- Stir in just enough cold water to bring the pastry together into a pliable dough then chill for 30 minutes.
- Preheat the oven to 200°C (180°C fan) / 400F / gas 6.
- Roll out the pastry on a floured surface and cut out 6 circles then use them to line 6 tartlet tins.
- Line the tins with clingfilm and fill with baking beans then bake for 10 minutes.
- Remove the film and beans and return the cases to the oven for 10 minutes or until cooked through and biscuity.

- Turn off the oven and preheat the grill.
- To make the filling, melt the butter in a small saucepan, then stir in the flour and cook over a medium heat until it forms a thick roux.
- Gradually stir in the alcohol free pale ale until it is all incorporated, then cook until thick.
- Stir in the Worcester sauce, mustard and cheese until the cheese melts into a thick paste.
- Spoon the rarebit mixture into the pastry cases and lay a slice of tomato on top of each one.
- Put the tartlets under the grill for 5 minutes or until golden brown and bubbling before sprinkling with chopped pine nuts.

Chicken Salad Flatbreads

Serves: 4   Preparation time: 10 minutes   Cooking time: 6 minutes

Ingredients

- 2 skinless chicken breasts
- 2 tbsp olive oil
- 4 flatbreads
- 4 tbsp mayonnaise
- 4 large lettuce leaves
- ½ red onion, peeled and sliced
- 2 medium tomatoes, sliced

- Cut each chicken breast diagonally into 6 pieces and brush with olive oil.

- Heat a griddle pan on the hob until very hot then fry the chicken pieces for 3 minutes on each side.

- Put a flatbread onto each plate and spread with half of the mayonnaise.

- Lay a lettuce leaf on each one and scatter over the onion and tomato.

- Lay 3 pieces of chicken on top of each flatbread and spoon over the rest of the mayonnaise.

- Fold over the sides of each flatbread and secure with a cocktail stick.

Top Tip

Add a few drops of Tabasco and a pinch of chili flakes when cooking the chicken for a touch of spice.

Tasty lunchtime treat!

Top Tip

Add 2 chopped rashers of smoky bacon, or a diced cooked chicken breast for a more meaty texture.

Super-healthy lunch.

Caesar Salad

Serves: 4 Preparation time: 10 minutes Cooking time: 5–8 minutes

Ingredients

- 2 thick slices of white bread
- 4 tbsp olive oil
- 50 g / 1 ¾ oz / ⅓ cup Parmesan
- 8 anchovy fillets in oil, drained
- 1 cos lettuce, leaves separated and washed
- a small bunch chives

For the dressing:
- 4 tbsp mayonnaise
- ½ clove of garlic, crushed
- 1 anchovy fillet, finely chopped
- 1 tbsp Parmesan, finely grated

- Preheat the oven to 190°C (170°C fan) / 375F / gas 5.

- Brush the bread with oil on both sides then cut off and discard the crusts. Cut the bread into cubes and spread them out on a baking tray.

- Bake the croutons in the oven for 5–8 minutes or until crisp and golden. Transfer to a wire rack to cool.

- Use a vegetable peeler to shave the Parmesan into thin slices.

- Cut the anchovy fillets into short lengths.

- Cut the lettuce across into thick ribbons and toss it with the Parmesan shavings and anchovies. Scatter over the croutons and chives.

- To make a classic Caesar dressing to serve alongside, mix the mayonnaise with the garlic, chopped anchovy and grated parmesan.

Lemon Chicken Goujons

Serves: 4 **Preparation time:** 35 minutes **Cooking time:** 4–5 minutes

Ingredients

- 4 skinless chicken breasts
- 1 lemon, zest and juice
- 4 tbsp plain flour
- 1 egg, beaten
- 75 g / 2 ½ oz / ¾ cup breadcrumbs
- 2 litres / 8 ½ cups / 3 ½ pints sunflower oil

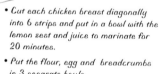
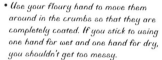

- Cut each chicken breast diagonally into 6 strips and put in a bowl with the lemon zest and juice to marinate for 20 minutes.

- Put the flour, egg and breadcrumbs in 3 separate bowls.

- Drain the chicken and dry well with kitchen paper.

- Dip the pieces in the flour with one hand and pat off any excess, then drop them into the beaten egg.

- Take them out of the egg with your other hand and drop them into the breadcrumbs.

- Use your floury hand to move them around in the crumbs so that they are completely coated. If you stick to using one hand for wet and one hand for dry, you shouldn't get too messy.

- Heat the oil in a deep fat fryer, according to the manufacturer's instructions, to a temperature of 180°C.

- Lower the goujons in the fryer basket and cook for 4–5 minutes or until crisp and golden brown. You may need to cook the chicken in 2 batches to avoid overcrowding the fryer, in which case keep the first batch warm in a low oven.

- Line a large bowl with a thick layer of kitchen paper and when they are ready, tip them into the bowl to remove any excess oil.

- Sprinkle with a little sea salt to taste and serve immediately.

Top Tip

Add 2 tbsp dried herbs
to the breadcrumbs,
for a more herby
flavour.

Great
side dish.

Macaroni cheese with bacon

Chicken burgers with cheese and coleslaw

Meal Time

Tuna minestrone

Yorkshire puddings

Top Tip

Mix 3 tsp of wholegrain mustard through the mashed potato for a more savoury flavour.

Serve with sausages.

Creamy Mashed Potato

Serves: 4   Preparation time: 2 minutes   Cooking time: 15 minutes

Ingredients

- 900 g / 2 lb / 5 ¼ cups potatoes, peeled and cubed
- 250 ml / 9 fl. oz / 1 cup whole milk
- 150 g / 5 ½ oz / ⅔ cups butter, cubed

- Put the potatoes in a pan of cold, salted water and bring to the boil.
- Cook the potatoes for 10 minutes or until tender all the way through.
- Tip the potatoes into a colander and leave to drain.
- Put the saucepan back on the heat and add the milk and butter.
- Heat until the milk starts to simmer then return the potatoes to the pan.
- Take the pan off the heat and mash with a potato masher until smooth.
- Season to taste with salt and pepper and serve immediately.

Cauliflower Cheese

Serves: 4   Preparation time: 15 minutes   Cooking time: 15–20 minutes

Ingredients

- 1 small cauliflower
- 25 g / 1 oz / $\frac{1}{10}$ cup butter
- 25 g / 1 oz / $\frac{1}{4}$ cup plain flour
- 600 ml / 2 ½ cups / 1 pint milk
- 150 g / 5 ½ oz / 1 ½ cups
  Cheddar cheese, grated

- Preheat the oven to 200°C (180°C fan) / 400f / gas 6.

- Cut the cauliflower into quarters and remove the main stalk and any leaves.

- Break the rest into large florets and blanch for 5 minutes in boiling, lightly salted water. Drain well.

- Melt the butter in a medium saucepan then stir in the flour. Gradually whisk in the milk a little at a time until it is all incorporated.

- Cook the sauce over a low heat, stirring constantly, until the mixture thickens. Any lumps that form should disperse with some vigorous stirring.

- Take the pan off the heat and stir in half of the cheese. Season to taste with salt and pepper.

- Arrange the blanched cauliflower in a baking dish and pour over the cheese sauce.

- Sprinkle over the remaining cheese then bake for 15–20 minutes or until the top is golden brown and bubbling.

Top Tip

Substitute half the Cheddar cheese with crumbled Danish Blue cheese as a delicious alternative.

Baked cauliflower with melted cheese.

Top Tip

Season with a pinch of cayenne and smoked paprika mixed with some salt for a Southern-Fried flavour.

Goes with everything!

Home-made Chips

Serves: 4   Preparation time: 1 hour 45 minutes   Cooking time: 15 minutes

Ingredients

- 4 large floury potatoes
  (eg. Maris Piper or King Edwards)
- 2–3 litres / 8 ½–13 cups /
  3 ½ pints–5 pints sunflower oil

- Peel the potatoes and cut them into thick slices then cut each slice into fingers.

- Put the chips in a bowl of cold water and leave them to soak for 1 hour. This will remove some of the starch that would otherwise make them brown too quickly.

- Drain the chips and dry them really well with a clean tea towel, then spread them out on a wire rack to air-dry for 30 minutes. It is dangerous to let water mix with hot oil, so it is important to make sure that the chips are completely dry before moving on to the next stage.

- Heat the oil in a deep fat fryer, according to the manufacturer's instructions, to a temperature of 130°C.

- Lower the chips in the fryer basket and cook for 10 minutes so that they cook all the way through but don't brown.
  You may need to do this in batches so that the fryer isn't overcrowded.

- Pull up the fryer basket and drain the chips on plenty of kitchen paper to absorb the excess oil.

- Increase the fryer temperature to 190°C. When the oil has come up to temperature, lower the fryer basket and cook the chips for 4–5 minutes or until crisp and golden brown.

- Line a large bowl with a thick layer of kitchen paper and when the chips are ready, tip them into the bowl to remove any excess oil.

- Sprinkle with a little sea salt to taste and serve immediately.

Chilli Con Carne

Serves: 4   Preparation time: 2 minutes   Cooking time: 1 hour 15 minutes

Ingredients

- 2 tbsp olive oil
- 2 shallots, finely chopped
- 1 red chilli, finely chopped
- 2 cloves of garlic, crushed
- ½ tsp Cayenne pepper
- 450 g / 1 lb / 2 cups minced beef
- 1 red pepper, chopped
- 400 g / 14 oz / 1 ³/₄ cups canned tomatoes, chopped
- 400 ml / 14 fl. oz / 1 ³/₄ cup beef stock
- 400 g / 14 oz / 4 cups canned kidney beans, drained
- 2 tbsp coriander (cilantro) leaves, chopped

- Heat the oil in a large saucepan and fry the shallots and chilli for 3 minutes, stirring occasionally.

- Add the garlic and Cayenne and cook for 2 minutes, then add the mince.

- Fry the mince until it starts to brown then add the red peppers and stir-fry for 2 more minutes.

- Add the chopped tomatoes and stock and bring to a gentle simmer.

- Cook the chilli con carne for 1 hour, stirring occasionally, until the mince is tender and the sauce has thickened a little.

- Stir in the kidney beans and cook for 5 more minutes to heat through. Taste for seasoning and add salt and freshly ground black pepper.

- Garnish with the coriander just before serving.

Top Tip

Serve with a generous dollop of sour cream to balance the spiciness of the chilli.

Perfect winter-warmer.

Perfect for the whole family.

Vegetable Lasagne

Serves: 4   Preparation time: 20 minutes   Cooking time: 50 minutes

Ingredients

- 2 tbsp olive oil
- 1 red onion, finely chopped
- 1 red pepper, diced
- 2 cloves of garlic, crushed
- 1 courgette, (zucchini) cubed
- ½ head broccoli, chopped
- 200 g / 7 oz / 2 ½ cups of button mushrooms, sliced

- 100 g / 3 ½ oz / ⅓ cup of canned sweetcorn, drained
- 400 g / 14 oz / 1 ¾ cups of canned tomatoes, chopped
- 300 g / 10 ½ oz lasagne sheets
- 100 g / 3 ½ oz / 1 cup of Gruyere, grated

- Heat the oil in a large saucepan and fry the onion and red pepper for 3 minutes, stirring occasionally.
- Add the garlic and cook for 2 minutes, then add the rest of the vegetables and the canned tomatoes.
- Half-fill the can with water and add it to the pan then bring to the boil and simmer for 10 minutes.

- Preheat the oven to 190°C (170°C fan) / 375F / gas 5.
- Oil a large baking dish and add a quarter of the vegetable sauce.
- Top with a layer of pasta then continue layering until the sauce has been used up.
- Sprinkle the top layer of sauce with grated cheese and bake in the oven for 30 minutes or until cooked through and golden brown.

Chicken Burgers with Cheese and Coleslaw

Makes: 4   Preparation time: 35 minutes   Cooking time: 8 minutes

Ingredients

- 600 g / 1lb / 5 oz / 2 ²/₃ cups chicken thigh, chopped
- 1 clove of garlic, crushed
- 25 g / 1oz / ¼ cup of Parmesan, finely grated
- 2 tbsp olive oil

For the coleslaw:
- 1 carrot, peeled
- ¼ red cabbage
- 4 spring onions

- ½ lemon, juiced
- 4 tbsp mayonnaise

To finish:
- 4 burger buns, halved
- 100 g / 3 ½ oz / 1 cup grated cheese
- 1 spring onion, sliced

- To make the burgers, put all of the ingredients except the oil into a food processor and pulse until finely chopped and evenly mixed.

- Shape the mixture into 4 patties then chill for 30 minutes to firm up.

- Meanwhile, make the coleslaw. Coarsely grate the carrot and transfer to a large mixing bowl.

- Cut the cabbage and spring onions into very thin slices and mix with the grated carrot, breaking everything up into individual strands with your fingers.

- Stir the lemon juice into the mayonnaise and use it to dress the shredded vegetables.

- Taste the coleslaw for seasoning, adding salt and pepper as necessary.

- Heat the oil in a large frying pan and fry the burgers for 4 minutes on each side or until cooked through and golden brown.

- Put a big spoonful of coleslaw onto the bottom half of the burger buns and top each one with a burger.

- Top the burgers with grated cheese and a few slices of spring onion then sandwich together with the top half of the buns.

Top Tip

Add a finely chopped red chilli to the chicken mixture for a touch of spice.

Healthy burgers.

Top Tip

Add a thinly sliced red pepper to the stir-fry for more colour.

Sesame Chicken Noodles

Serves: 4   Preparation time: 5 minutes   Cooking time: 8 minutes

Ingredients

- 250 g / 9 oz / 3 ⅓ cups egg noodles
- 2 tbsp sunflower oil
- 2 chicken breasts, sliced
- 2 cloves garlic, finely chopped
- 2 cm (1 in) piece root ginger, finely chopped

- 200 g / 7 oz / 1 ⅓ cups mange tout, trimmed
- 1 carrot, grated
- 1 tbsp light soy sauce
- 1 tsp sesame oil
- 1 tbsp sesame seeds

- Cook the noodles in boiling salted water for 4 minutes then drain well and refresh in cold water. Drain again.

- Heat the sunflower oil in a large wok until very hot then fry the chicken pieces until lightly coloured on all sides.

- Add the garlic and ginger and cook for 1 minute then add the mange tout and cook for a further minute.

- Add the grated carrot and drained noodles to the pan with the soy sauce and stir-fry for 2 minutes to heat through.

- Stir in the sesame oil and seeds and serve immediately.

Rice Salad

Serves: 4   Preparation time: 30 minutes   Cooking time: 20 minutes

Ingredients

- 200 g / 7 oz / ⁴/₅ cups of basmati rice
- 100 g / 3 ½ oz / ¾ cup frozen peas
- 100 g / 3 ½ oz / ¾ of cup ham, cubed

For the dressing:
- 3 tbsp olive oil
- 1 lemon, juiced
- 1 tsp runny honey

- Soak the rice in cold water for 30 minutes then drain well.
- Put the rice in a medium saucepan and add enough water to cover by 1 cm.
- Bring the water to the boil then cover the pan tightly, reduce the heat to its lowest setting and cook for 10 minutes without disturbing.
- Turn off the heat and leave the rice to stand for 10 minutes without disturbing.

- Meanwhile, cook the peas in boiling water for 2 minutes then drain.
- Put the dressing ingredients in a small jar with a pinch of salt and shake well to mix.
- When the rice is ready, remove the lid and fluff up the grains with a fork.
- Carefully fold in the ham, peas and dressing then leave to cool to room temperature before serving.

Top Tip

Substitute the ham for cooked prawns (shrimps) or shredded crab as a seafood based alternative.

Great with chicken!

Top Tip

Swap the tuna steak for a cooked chicken breast diced to make a more meaty minestrone.

Serve with warm, crusty bread.

Tuna Minestrone

Serves: 4   Preparation time: 2 minutes   Cooking time: 25 minutes

Ingredients

- 2 tbsp olive oil
- 1 onion, finely chopped
- ½ celery stick, finely chopped
- 1 carrot, finely chopped
- 1 clove of garlic, crushed
- 2 medium tomatoes, peeled and chopped
- 1.2 litres / 2 pints / 5 cups of vegetable stock

- 75 g / 2 ½ oz / ¾ cup small pasta shapes
- 75 g / 2 ½ oz / ½ cup of French beans, chopped
- 100 g / 3 ½ oz / 1 ½ cups of canned kidney beans, drained
- 1 fresh tuna steak, cubed

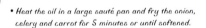

- Heat the oil in a large sauté pan and fry the onion, celery and carrot for 5 minutes or until softened.

- Add the garlic and cook for 2 more minutes, stirring constantly.

- Add the tomatoes and stock and bring to the boil then add the pasta shapes and cook for 8 minutes.

- Add the French beans and cook for 4 minutes then add the kidney beans and tuna steak and simmer for 2 minutes just to heat through.

- Taste the soup for seasoning and add salt and pepper as necessary.

Mediterranean Meatloaf

Serves: 8   Preparation time: 45 minutes   Cooking time: 2 hours

Ingredients

- 2 tbsp olive oil
- 1 onion, finely chopped
- 1 courgette (zucchini) finely chopped
- 1 orange pepper, chopped
- 1 clove of garlic, crushed
- 450 g / 1 lb / 2 cups of minced beef
- 450 g / 1 lb / 2 cups of pork sausage meat
- 50 g / 1 ³/₄ oz / ½ cup of fresh white breadcrumbs
- 2 tbsp pine nuts
- 1 tbsp sultanas
- 1 tbsp fresh thyme leaves
- 1 large egg, beaten

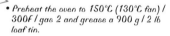

- Preheat the oven to 150°C (130°C fan) / 300F / gas 2 and grease a 900 g / 2 lb loaf tin.

- Heat the oil in a large sauté pan and fry the onion, courgette and pepper together for 10 minutes or until softened.

- Add the garlic and cook for 2 more minutes, stirring constantly, then scrape the mixture into a large mixing bowl and leave to cool.

- Add the rest of the ingredients and squidge it all together with your hands until it is really well mixed.

- Pack the meat into the prepared loaf tin and cover the top with foil.

- Put it in a large roasting tin and add enough boiling water to come half way up the outside of the loaf tin. This is called a bain-marie and will help the meatloaf to cook evenly without hardening on the outside.

- Transfer the bain-marie to the oven and cook for 2 hours.

- To test if it is done, insert a skewer into the centre of the meatloaf. Take it out then press down on the top of the loaf. If the juices run clear, it is cooked.

- Cover the meatloaf with foil again and leave to rest for 20 minutes before turning out onto a serving plate and serving warm.

- Alternatively, leave the meatloaf to cool completely in the tin then refrigerate. Serve cold in a packed lunch or at a picnic.

Top Tip

Add a finely chopped green chilli for a mild spicy kick.

Serve with warm green veg.

Top Tip

Add a small handful of thinly sliced mushrooms to the pasta and sauce to vary the texture.

Macaroni Cheese with Bacon

Serves: 4   Preparation time: 20 minutes   Cooking time: 50 minutes

Ingredients

- 400 g / 14 oz / 4 cups of dried macaroni
- 25 g / 1 oz / ¹/₁₀ cup of butter
- 4 rashers streaky bacon, chopped
- 25 g / 1 oz / ¹/₁₀ cup plain flour
- 600 ml / 1 pint / 2 ½ cups of milk
- 150 g / 5 ½ oz / 1 ½ cups of Cheddar
  cheese, grated

- Preheat the oven to 180°C (160°C fan) / 350F / gas 4.
- Cook the macaroni in boiling, salted water for 10 minutes or until almost cooked. Drain well.
- Meanwhile, melt the butter in a medium saucepan then fry the bacon for 2 minutes. Stir in the flour.
- Gradually whisk in the milk a little at a time until it is all incorporated.

- Cook the sauce over a low heat, stirring constantly, until the mixture thickens. Any lumps that form should disperse with some vigorous stirring.
- Take the pan off the heat and stir in half of the cheese. Season to taste with salt and pepper.
- Stir the macaroni into the cheese sauce and scrape it into a baking dish.
- Sprinkle over the remaining cheese then bake for 45 minutes or until the top is golden brown and the pasta is cooked.

Braised Beef with Carrots

Serves: 4   Preparation time: 30 minutes   Cooking time: 3 hours

Ingredients

- 400 g / 14 oz / 2 ½ cups of braising steak
- 2 tbsp plain flour
- 1 tsp mustard powder
- 4 tbsp olive oil

- 1 onion, finely chopped
- 4 carrots, sliced
- 2 sprigs fresh rosemary
- 4 sprigs fresh thyme
- 1 litre / 2 pints / 5 cups of good quality beef stock

- Preheat the oven to 140° C (120°C fan) / 275F / gas 1.

- Cut each steak into 3 or 4 large pieces. Mix the flour with the mustard powder and a good pinch of salt and pepper and tip it into a large freezer bag. Add the pieces of beef, seal the bag and shake it around to coat the meat evenly.

- Heat half of the oil in a large cast iron casserole dish until very hot. Sear the meat all over in batches so that it is nicely browned on the outside then transfer it to a plate.

- Add the rest of the oil to the pan and lower the heat a little then cook the onions for 5 minutes or until softened but not browned.

- Return the meat to the pan with the carrots, herbs and stock and bring to a gentle simmer.

- Put a lid on the casserole and transfer it to the oven to cook for 3 hours, stirring every hour.

- When the time is up, make sure that the meat is tender and taste the sauce for seasoning. Adjust with salt and pepper as necessary.

- Spoon the casserole into a warm serving dish before taking it to the table.

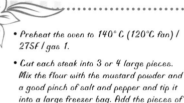

Top Tip

Swap ½ the carrots for a sweet potato, peeled and cut into cubes for a sweeter taste.

Perfect for cold days.

Top Tip

Put a teaspoon of sausage meat into the centre of each the Yorkshire pudding before cooking, for a tasty meat filled alternative.

For roast dinners!

Yorkshire Puddings

Makes: 6   Preparation time: 5 minutes   Cooking time: 25 minutes

Ingredients

- 2 tbsp sunflower oil
- 75 g / 2 ½ oz / ³/₄ cup of plain flour
- 2 large eggs
- 100 ml / 3 ½ fl. oz / ¹/₃ cup of whole milk

- Preheat the oven to 230° C (210°C fan / 450f / gas 8.
- Put a teaspoon of oil into each hole of a deep 6-hole muffin tin and put it in the oven to heat.
- Put the flour in a large jug with a pinch of salt and make a well in the centre.
- Break in the eggs and pour in the milk then use a whisk to gradually incorporate all of the flour from round the outside.
- Carefully take the muffin tin out of the oven and immediately divide the batter between the holes.
- Return the tin to the oven and bake for 25 minutes without opening the oven door.
- Serve straight away.

Pasta and Meatballs in Tomato Sauce

Serves: 6   Preparation time: 30 minutes   Cooking time: 50 minutes

Ingredients

- 4 tbsp olive oil
- 1 onion, finely chopped
- 1 clove of garlic, crushed
- 250 g / 9 oz / 1 cup of minced beef
- 250 g / 9 oz / 1 cup of pork sausage meat

- 50 g / 1 ³/₄ oz / ½ cup of fresh white breadcrumbs
- 1 tbsp fresh thyme leaves
- 1 egg yolk
- 600 ml / 1 pint / 2 ½ cups of tomato passata
- 600 g / 1 lb 4 oz / 6 cups of long pasta (eg. spaghetti or tagliatelle)
- 6 sprigs fresh basil

- Heat half of the oil in a large sauté pan and fry the onion for 5 minutes or until softened.

- Add the garlic and cook for 2 more minutes, stirring constantly, then scrape the mixture into a large mixing bowl and leave to cool.

- Add the mince, sausage meat, breadcrumbs, thyme and egg yolk and squidge it all together with your hands until it is really well mixed.

- Use an ice cream scoop to portion the mixture into evenly sized pieces then roll them in your hands to form firm meatballs.

- Heat the rest of the oil in the sauté pan and sear the meatballs on all sides. This should take around 10 minutes.

- Pour over the tomato passata and simmer gently for 30 minutes or until the meatballs are cooked all the way through and the sauce has thickened a little.

- Keep the pan on a low heat while you boiling the pasta.

- Cook the pasta in a very large saucepan of boiling, salted water according to the packet instructions. This usually varies between 5 minutes and 12 minutes.

- Drain the pasta and divide between 6 warm bowls then spoon over the meatballs and sauce.

- Garnish with basil before serving.

Top Tip

Substitute the minced beef for minced chicken for a lighter more healthy option.

Serve with extra cheese!

Top Tip

Add 2 tsp of creamed horseradish to the mashed potatoes and mix, for a more spicy finish.

Perfect for the whole family.

Cottage Pie

Serves: 4   **Preparation time:** 10 minutes   **Cooking time:** 1 hour 30 minutes

Ingredients

- 2 tbsp olive oil
- 1 small onion, finely chopped
- 2 cloves of garlic, crushed
- 450 g / 1 lb / 2 cups of minced beef
- 400 g / 14 oz / 1 ¾ cups of canned tomatoes, chopped
- 400 ml / 14 fl. oz / 1 ¾ cups of beef stock

For the topping:
- 450 g / 1 lb / 2 ½ cups of floury potatoes, peeled and cubed
- 100 ml / 3 ½ fl. oz / ⅓ cup of milk
- 50 g / 1 ¾ oz / ⅕ cup of butter
- 50 g / 1 ¾ oz / ½ cup of cheese, grated

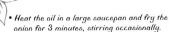

- Heat the oil in a large saucepan and fry the onion for 3 minutes, stirring occasionally.
- Add the garlic and cook for 2 minutes, then add the mince.
- Fry the mince until it starts to brown then add the chopped tomatoes and stock and bring to a gentle simmer.
- Cook for 1 hour, stirring occasionally, until the mince is tender and the sauce has thickened a little.
- Taste for seasoning and add salt and freshly ground black pepper as necessary.

- Meanwhile, cook the potatoes in salted water for 10 minutes, or until they are tender, then drain well.
- Return the potatoes to the saucepan and add the milk and butter. Mash the potatoes until smooth.
- Preheat the oven to 200°C (180° fan), 400f, gas 6.
- Spoon the mince mixture into a large baking dish then top with the mashed potatoes.
- Use a fork to level the surface and make stripes in the potato.
- Sprinkle over the grated cheese and bake in the oven for 20 minutes or until golden brown.

Fish Fingers

Serves: 4   Preparation time: 15 minutes   Cooking time: 4–5 minutes

Ingredients

- 800 g / 1 lb 12 oz / 4 cups of pollock fillet
- 4 tbsp plain flour
- 1 egg, beaten
- 75 g / 2 ½ oz / ³/₄ cup of breadcrumbs
- 2 litres / 3 ½ pints / 8 ½ cups of sunflower oil

- Cut the fish into 16 evenly sized finger shapes.
- Put the flour, egg and panko breadcrumbs in 3 separate bowls.
- Dip the fish fingers in the flour with one hand and pat off any excess, then drop them into the beaten egg.
- Take them out of the egg with your other hand and drop them into the breadcrumbs.
- Use your floury hand to move them around in the crumbs so that they are completely coated. If you stick to using one hand for wet and one hand for dry, you shouldn't get too messy.

- Heat the oil in a deep fat fryer, according to the manufacturer's instructions, to a temperature of 180° C.
- Lower the fish fingers in the fryer basket and cook for 4–5 minutes or until crisp and golden brown. You may need to cook them in 2 batches to avoid overcrowding the fryer, in which case keep the first batch warm in a low oven.
- Line a large bowl with a thick layer of kitchen paper and when they are ready, tip them into the bowl to remove any excess oil.
- Sprinkle with a little sea salt to taste and serve immediately.

Top Tip

Add some lemon zest and black pepper to the breadcrumbs for a zest variation.

Make extra and freeze them!

Top Tip

Add 2 cooked smoked bacon rashers chopped into lardons to the dish for an extra salty bite.

Serve with salad.

Macaroni Cheese Frittata

Serves: 4   Preparation time: 5 minutes   Cooking time: 20 minutes

Ingredients

- 100 g / 3 ½ oz / 1 cup of dried macaroni
- 5 large eggs, beaten
- 150 g / 5 ½ oz / 1 ½ cups of cheese, grated
- 2 tbsp basil leaves, chopped
- 1 tbsp olive oil

- Preheat the oven to 180° C (160°C fan) / 350F / gas 4.
- Cook the macaroni in boiling, salted water for 12 minutes or until al dente. Drain well and leave to cool a little.
- Stir in the beaten eggs, half the cheese and the chopped basil then season with salt and pepper.
- Preheat the grill to its highest setting.

- Heat the oil in an oven-proof frying pan and swirl to coat, then pour in the omelette mixture and level the surface.
- Cook over a low heat for 4 minutes or until the outside has set, then sprinkle over the rest of the cheese.
- Put the frying pan under the grill and cook for 3 more minutes or until the top is golden and the centre is set.
- Serve plain or topped with grilled bacon.

Fresh Tomato Soup

Serves: 4   Preparation time: 5 minutes   Cooking time: 25 minutes

Ingredients

- 900 g / 2 lb / 4 ½ cups of large ripe tomatoes
- 2 tbsp olive oil
- 1 onion, finely chopped
- 2 cloves of garlic, crushed
- 500 ml / 18 fl. oz / 2 ¼ cups of vegetable stock

- 150 ml / 5 ½ fl. oz / ⅔ cup of double cream
- a few sprigs basil

- Score a cross in the top of each tomato then lower them into a large pan of boiling water. Cook for 30 seconds, or until the skin by the cross just starts to curl up, then remove the tomatoes with a slotted spoon and plunge into iced water. Depending on the size of your pan, you may need to do this in batches.

- When the tomatoes are cool enough to handle, peel off and discard the skins. Cut the tomatoes in half and scrape the seeds into a sieve set over a bowl. Discard the seeds, but reserve the any juice that comes out.

- Cut the peeled and deseeded tomatoes into small cubes.

- Heat the oil in a large saucepan and fry the onion for 5 minutes or until softened.

- Add the garlic and cook for 2 more minutes, stirring constantly.

- Add the tomatoes, stock and reserved tomato juice and bring to the boil then simmer for 20 minutes.

- Add half of the cream and use a stick blender to blend until smooth.

- Taste the soup for seasoning and adjust with salt and pepper as necessary.

- Ladle into warm bowls and garnish with an extra swirl of cream and some fresh basil leaves.

Top Tip

Add 4 tbsp cooked pasta shells into the soup to give it some texture.

Serve with crusty bread.

Hazelnut and cinnamon muffins

Jam biscuits

Sweets

Chocolate truffles

Chocolate and Cherry Cupcakes

Top Tip

Spice up the pie with a couple of cloves and ½ a teaspoon of allspice, and add 3 tbsp raisins for a fruity kick.

Perfect for the whole family.

Apple Pie

Serves: 6-8   Preparation time: 45 minutes   Cooking time: 40 minutes

Ingredients

- 800 g / 2lb / 8 cups of bramley apples
- 125 g/ 4 ½ / ½ cup of caster sugar
- 2 tbsp plain flour
- ½ tsp ground cinnamon

- 1 egg, beaten

For the pastry:
- 300 g / 10 ½ oz / 3 cups of plain flour
- 150 g / 5 ½ oz / 1 ²/₃ cup of butter, chilled

- To make the pastry, sieve the flour into a bowl to remove any lumps.
- Dip the chilled butter in the flour then grate it into the bowl. Use a fork to mix the butter evenly with the flour.
- To make the mixture into a dough you need to add cold water a little at a time.
- As soon as it feels like playdough, wrap the ball in clingfilm and leave it to rest in the fridge for 30 minutes.
- Preheat the oven to 190°C (170°C fan) / 375f / gas 5 and butter a 20 cm round pie tin.
- Peel the apples then cut them into quarters and remove the core with a paring knife.
- Cut the apples into evenly-sized chunks then use a clean tea towel to blot away any excess moisture, this could make your pastry soggy.
- Mix the sugar, flour and cinnamon together in a bowl then add the apples and mix together.
- Take the pastry out of the fridge and divide it into 2 pieces.
- Dust the work surface and a rolling pin with flour.

- Roll out the pastry until you have a large sheet of pastry that is 5mm thick all over, use your rolling pin to help you transfer it to the pie tin. Press the pastry into the base and let the edges hang down the sides.
- Pack the apples into the pastry case and brush around the top of the pastry with beaten egg.
- Roll out the other half of the pastry the same way as before to make the lid.
- Lay the pastry over the apples and press down round the outside to seal.
- Use a pair of scissors to cut away the excess pastry, leaving a 2 cm border.
- Use a knife to make a hole in the middle of the lid for the steam to escape then brush the top of the pie with beaten egg.
- Put the pie in the oven and bake for 40 minutes - the pastry should be crisp and golden brown on top and starting to shrink away from the edge of the tin.
- Leave the pie to cool for 15 minutes, then cut into slices and serve warm.

Raspberry and Vanilla Trifle Pots

Serves: 6   Preparation time: 20 minutes   Cooking time: 15–20 minutes

Ingredients

- 200 g / 7 oz / 1 ³/₄ cups of raspberries
- 1 small Madeira loaf cake

For the custard:
- 1 vanilla pod, split lengthways
- 450 ml / 16 fl. oz / 1 ³/₄ cups of whole milk
- 4 large egg yolks
  75 g / 2 ½ oz / 1 ¹/₃ cup of caster sugar
  2 tsp cornflour

- To make the custard, scrape the seeds out of the vanilla pod and put them in a small saucepan with the milk. Bring the milk gently to a simmer then turn off the heat and leave it to infuse with the vanilla for 5 minutes.

- Whisk the egg yolks, sugar and cornflour together in a mixing bowl then gradually whisk in the milk.

- Scrape the mixture back into the saucepan then cook over a medium heat until the mixture thickens, stirring constantly.

- Take the pan off the heat and sit the base in cold water to stop the custard from cooking any further.

- Put one third of the raspberries in a small bowl and mash them with a fork. Stir in the whole raspberries.

- Put a spoonful of the raspberry mixture in the bottom of 6 glasses and crumble over half of the cake.

- Divide half of the custard between the glasses then add half of the remaining raspberries.

- Top with the rest of the cake, then the rest of the custard and finish each glass with a ring of raspberries around the outside.

- You can also cut the empty vanilla pod into thin strips to decorate the tops of the trifle pots, but these should be removed before eating.

Top Tip

Add 3 tbsp of chopped hazelnuts to the mixture for a delicious nutty taste and texture.

Perfect to share.

Fudge

Makes: 36 pieces   *Cooking time: 45 minutes*

Ingredients

- 300 ml / 10 ½ fl. oz / 1 ¼ cup of whole milk
- 100 g / 3 ½ oz / ½ cup of butter
- 350 g / 12 oz / 1 ½ cups of caster sugar

- Oil an 18 cm x 18 cm square cake tin.

- Put the milk, butter and caster sugar in a large, heavy-based saucepan and stir over a low heat to dissolve the sugar.

- Increase the temperature a little and bring to the boil.

- Boil the mixture for 35 minutes or until the mixture reaches 115°C on a sugar thermometer. It is important to stir the mixture constantly as this will stop it from burning on the bottom and it will give the fudge a nice crumbly texture.

- When the time is up, take the pan off the heat and continue to stir for 10 minutes while it cools.

- Scrape the mixture into the prepared tin and level the surface with a palate knife.

- When the fudge has cooled completely to room temperature it should be set solid.

- Turn it out of the tin in one piece and cut into squares with a sharp knife.

- The fudge mixture will stay hot for a long time, so don't be tempted to try any of the liquid mixture in the pan.

Lemon Loaf Cake

Serves: 12   Preparation time: 10 minutes   Cooking time: 35–40 minutes

Ingredients

- 150 g / 5 ½ oz / 1 ¼ cups of self-raising flour
- 150 g / 5 ½ oz / ⅔ cup of caster sugar
- 150 g / 5 ½ oz / ⅔ cup of butter
- 3 eggs
- 1 tsp baking powder

- 1 tbsp lemon zest
- 2 tbsp lemon juice

To decorate:
- 200 g / 7 oz / 1 ½ cups of icing (confectioner's) sugar
- 2–4 tsp lemon juice
- 3 lemon slices

- Preheat the oven to 180°C (160°C fan) / 350F / gas 4 and grease and line a small loaf tin.
- Put all of the cake ingredients in a bowl and whisk them together with an electric whisk for 4 minutes or until pale and well whipped.
- Scrape the mixture into the tin and level the top with a spatula.
- Bake for 35–40 minutes. The cake is ready when a toothpick inserted into the centre comes out clean.
- Transfer the cake to a wire rack to cool completely.
- To make the icing, sift the icing sugar then stir in the lemon juice a few drops at a time until you have a thick icing. Spread it on top of the cake with a palette knife.
- Garnish the cake with fresh lemon slices just before serving.

Top Tip

Add 2 tsp of poppy seeds into the cake mixture, to make a more interesting texture with a slightly nutty flavour.

Great for entertaining!

Top Tip

Mix in 3 tbsp of golden raisins before cooking for a sweet fruity taste.

Easy and tasty!

Cinnamon Rice Pudding

Serves: 4   Preparation time: 5 minutes   Cooking time: 1 hour 30 minutes

Ingredients

- 50 g / 2 oz / ¹/₅ cup of butter
- 110 g / 4 oz / ½ cup of short-grain rice
- 75 g / 2 ½ oz / ¹/₃ cup of caster sugar
- 2 tsp ground cinnamon
- 1.2 litres / 2 pints / 5 cups of whole milk

- Preheat the oven to 140°C (120°C fan) / 275F / gas 1.
- Melt the butter in a cast iron casserole dish and add the rice, sugar and cinnamon.
- Stir over a low heat for 2 minutes then gradually incorporate the milk and bring to a simmer.
- Cover the casserole dish and bake in the oven for 1 hour, then remove the lid and cook for a further 30 minutes.
- The rice pudding can either be served hot at this stage or alternatively, spoon the rice into 4 sundae glasses and chill in the fridge before serving cold.

Blueberry Pancakes

Serves: 4   Preparation time: 10 minutes   Cooking time: 30 minutes

Ingredients

- 250 g / 9 oz / 2 ½ cups of plain flour
- 2 tsp baking powder
- 2 large eggs
- 300 ml / 10 ½ fl. oz / 1 ¼ cup of milk

- 25 g / 1 oz / ¹/₁₀ cup of butter, melted
- 150 g / 5 ½ oz / 1 ½ cups of blueberries
- 4 tsp butter
- 4 tbsp maple syrup

- Mix the flour and baking powder in a bowl and make a well in the centre.

- Break in the eggs and pour in the milk then use a whisk to gradually incorporate all of the flour from round the outside.

- Melt the butter in a small frying pan then whisk it into the batter.

- Put the buttered frying pan back over a low heat. You will need a table spoon of batter for each pancake and you should be able to cook 4 pancakes at a time in the frying pan.

- Spoon the batter into the pan and dot the tops with blueberries.

- Cook the pancakes for 2 minutes or until small bubbles start to appear on the surface of the pancakes.

- Turn the pancakes over with a spatula and cook the other side until golden brown and cooked through.

- Repeat until all the batter has been used, keeping the finished batches warm in a low oven.

- Pile the pancakes onto warm plates and finish each one with a tsp of butter and a drizzle of maple syrup.

Top Tip

Try using other fruits and berries such as redcurrants, blackcurrants or chopped strawberries to vary the flavours.

Can be a breakfast treat too!

Top Tip

Substitute the blueberries for raspberries to change the colour and flavour of the topping.

Super impressive!

Blueberry Cheesecake

Serves: 10–12   **Preparation time:** 25 minutes   **Cooking time:** 40–50 minutes

Ingredients

- 200 g / 7 oz / 2 cups biscuits, crushed
- 50 g / 2 oz / 1/s cup of butter, melted
- 600 g / 1 lb 5 oz / 2 ½ cups of cream cheese
- 150 ml / 5 fl. oz / 2/3 cup of soured cream
- 175 g / 6 oz / 3/4 cup of caster sugar

- 2 large eggs
- 1 egg yolk
- 2 tbsp plain flour
- 1 tsp vanilla extract

For the blueberry topping:
- 3 sheets gelatine
- 200 g / 7 oz / 2 cups of blueberries
- 4 tbsp caster sugar

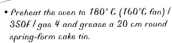

- Preheat the oven to 180°C (160°C fan) / 350F / gas 4 and grease a 20 cm round spring-form cake tin.
- Mix the biscuit crumbs with the butter and press into an even layer in the bottom of the tin.
- Bake the biscuit layer for 5 minutes or until firm.
- Whisk together the remaining ingredients until smooth.
- Spoon the cheesecake mixture on top of the biscuit base, levelling the top with a palette knife.
- Bake the cheesecake for 40–50 minutes or until the centre is only just set.
- Leave to cool completely in the tin.

- To make the topping, put the gelatine sheets into a shallow bowl and add enough cold water to cover. Leave to soak for 10 minutes.
- Put the blueberries in a small saucepan with the sugar and 2 tablespoons of water.
- Cover the pan and cook for a few minutes until the blueberries start to soften and burst. Take the pan off the heat.
- Squeeze the water out of the softened gelatine sheets then whisk them into the hot blueberry mixture to dissolve.
- Pour the blueberry jelly into the cheesecake tin to form a thin even layer on top.
- Transfer the tin to the fridge and chill for 2 hours before carefully unmoulding and serving.

Chocolate Truffles

Makes: 24   Preparation time: 30 minutes   Chilling time: 4 hours

Ingredients

- 165 ml / 6 fl. oz / ²/₃ cup of double cream
- 185 g / 6 ½ oz / 1 cup of dark chocolate
- 35 g / 1 ¼ oz / ¹/₁₀ cup of butter, softened
- 50 g / 1 ¾ oz / ½ cup of unsweetened cocoa powder

- Heat the cream until it starts to simmer.

- Break the chocolate into squares and pour over the hot cream, then stir gently to combine.

- Leave the ganache to cool a little then stir in the butter.

- If the ganache isn't smooth at this stage, use a stick blender to emulsify the mixture.

- Chill the ganache in the fridge for 4 hours or overnight.

- Sift the cocoa onto a plate.

- Use a melon baller dipped in cocoa to scoop the mixture into balls then roll them in the cocoa with the help of a couple of forks.

- Return to the fridge for 1 hour to firm up and serve chilled or at room temperature.

Make a great gift!

Top Tip

Add a nutty twist to the cake toppings by sprinkling some flaked almonds over the icing.

Perfect for picnics!

Chocolate and Cherry Cupcakes

Makes: 12   **Preparation time: 25 minutes**   **Cooking time: 15–20 minutes**

Ingredients

- 100 g / 3 ½ oz / 1 cup of self-raising flour, sifted
- 25 g / 1 oz / ¼ cup of unsweetened cocoa powder, sifted
- 100 g / 3 ½ oz / ½ cup of caster sugar
- 100 g / 3 ½ oz / ½ cup of butter, softened

- 3 large eggs
- 4 tbsp cherry jam
- 225 ml / 8 fl. oz / 1 cup of double cream
- 2 tbsp icing sugar
- ½ tsp vanilla extract
- 12 glacé cherries
- 55 g / 2 oz / ⅓ cup of milk chocolate, chilled

- Preheat the oven to 190°C (170°C fan) / 375F / gas 5 and line a 12-hole cupcake tin with paper cases.
- Combine the flour, cocoa, sugar, butter, eggs and jam in a bowl and whisk together for 2 minutes or until smooth.
- Divide the mixture between the paper cases, then transfer the tin to the oven and bake for 15–20 minutes.
- Test with a wooden toothpick, if it comes out clean, the cakes are done.

- Transfer the cakes to a wire rack and leave to cool completely.
- Whip the cream with the icing sugar and vanilla until thick then spoon it into a piping bag fitted with a large star nozzle.
- Pipe a rosette of cream on top of each cake then top each one with a cherry.
- Use a vegetable peeler to make thin curls from the chocolate and sprinkle over the cakes.

Jam Biscuits

Makes: 36   Preparation time: 1 hour 15 minutes   Cooking time: 25–30 minutes

Ingredients

- 150 g / 5 ½ oz / ²/₃ cup of caster sugar
- 350 g / 12 oz / 1 ½ cups of butter, softened
- 1 tsp vanilla extract
- 300 g / 10 ½ oz / 3 cups of plain flour
- 150 g / 5 ½ oz / 1 cup of ground almonds
- 1 jar strawberry jam

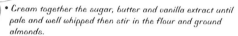

- Cream together the sugar, butter and vanilla extract until pale and well whipped then stir in the flour and ground almonds.

- Bring the mixture together into a ball with your hands then wrap in clingfilm and refrigerate for 45 minutes.

- Preheat the oven to 140°C (120°C fan) / 275F / gas 1 and line 2 baking sheets with greaseproof paper.

- Roll out the dough on a lightly floured surface to 5 mm thick. Use a fluted pastry cutter to cut out 72 biscuits, rerolling the trimmings as necessary.

- Use a small star cutter to cut the centre out of 36 of the biscuits.

- Transfer the biscuits to the prepared trays in batches and bake for 25–30 minutes or until cooked through and only just golden.

- Transfer the biscuits to a wire rack and leave to cool completely.

- Put a teaspoon of jam on the underside of the plain rounds and sandwich each one with a star biscuit.

A super lunchbox treat.

Perfect to share!

Hazelnut and Cinnamon Muffins

Makes: 12   Preparation time: 25 minutes   Cooking time: 20–25 minutes

Ingredients

- 1 large egg
- 120 ml / 4 fl. oz / ½ cup sunflower oil
- 120 ml / 4 fl. oz / ½ cup milk
- 375 g / 12 ½ oz / 3 ¾ cup self-raising flour, sifted

- 1 tsp baking powder
- 200 g / 7 oz / ¾ cup caster sugar
- 2 tsp ground cinnamon
- 100 g / 3 ½ oz / ½ cup hazelnuts (cobnuts), chopped

- Preheat the oven to 180°C (160°C fan) / 350F / gas 4 and line a 12-hole muffin tin with paper cases.

- Beat the egg in a jug with the oil and milk until well mixed.

- Mix the flour, baking powder, sugar, cinnamon and half of the chopped hazelnuts in a bowl.

- Pour in the egg mixture and stir just enough to combine.

- Divide the mixture between the paper cases and sprinkle over the reserved hazelnuts.

- Bake the muffins in the oven for 20–25 minutes.

- Test with a wooden toothpick, if it comes out clean, the cakes are done.

- Transfer the muffins to a wire rack and leave to cool completely.

Sultana Sponge with Lemon Buttercream

Serves: 12   Preparation time: 10 minutes   Cooking time: 35–40 minutes

Ingredients

- 200 g / 7 oz / 2 cups self-raising flour
- 200 g / 7 oz / 1 cup caster sugar
- 200 g / 7 oz / 1 cup butter
- 4 eggs
- 1 tsp baking powder

- 75 g / 2 ½ oz / ½ cup sultanas

To decorate:
- 100 g / 3 ½ oz / ½ cup butter, softened
- 200 g / 7 oz / 1 ½ cups icing sugar, plus extra for dusting
- ½ lemon, zest and juice

- Preheat the oven to 180°C (160°C fan), 350F, gas 4 and grease and line 2 x 20 cm round loose-bottomed cake tins.

- Put all of the cake ingredients in a large mixing bowl and whisk them together with an electric whisk for 4 minutes or until pale and well whipped.

- Divide the mixture between the two tins and level the tops with a spatula.

- Bake for 35–40 minutes. The cakes are ready when a toothpick comes out clean.

- Transfer the cakes to a wire rack to cool completely.

- To make the buttercream, whisk the butter with an electric whisk then gradually add the icing sugar. Add the lemon zest and juice and whisk until smooth.

- Spoon the buttercream into a piping bag fitted with a large star nozzle and pipe the icing on top of one of the cakes.

- Position the other cake on top and dust with icing sugar.

Top Tip

Substitute the lemon and juice for ½ an orange (zest and juice) for an alternative citrus zing.

Impress the family!

Index

Index